Hannelore Schäl
Sabine Lohf

Making Things With Yarn

Hannelore Schäl
Sabine Lohf

Making Things
With Yarn

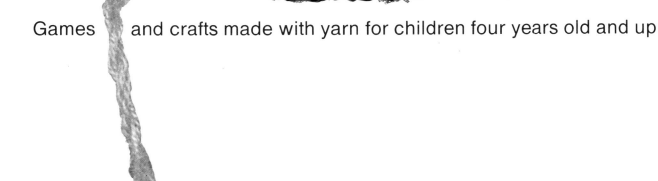

Games   and crafts made with yarn for children four years old and up

CHILDRENS PRESS®
CHICAGO

Translation by Mrs. Werner Lippmann and Mrs. Ruth Bookey

Library of Congress Cataloging-in-Publication Data

Schäl, Hannelore.
   [Ich mach was mit Wolle.   English]
   Making things with yarn : games and crafts made with yarn for
children four years old and up / by Hannelore Schäl, Sabine Lohf.
      p.   cm.
   Translation of: Ich mach was mit Wolle.
   Instructions for making a variety of art projects and decorations out of yarn.
   ISBN 0-516-09255-3
    1. Textile crafts—Juvenile literature.   2. Yarn—Juvenile
literature.   [1. Textile crafts.   2. Yarn.   3. Handicraft.]
I. Lohf, Sabine.   II. Title.
TT712.S3313   1989
746'.028—dc20
                                    89-22254
                                        CIP
                                        AC

Published in the United States in 1990 by Childrens Press®, Inc.,
5440 North Cumberland Avenue, Chicago, IL 60656.

CONTENTS

You will need:

Yarn, cotton batting, burlap, rope, a rug remnant or felt, wrapping paper, glue, thread, scissors

Sometimes a thick yarn has lots of smaller threads.

First try out various methods.

Tear off some pieces of cotton. Press the pieces together to make a cotton ball and flatten it into a cloud shape. This can be the cloud for your picture. Now try twirling some cotton between your fingers to make a cotton rope.

My untwisted yarn looks like a tree.

Make patterns or pictures with the rope, thread, and cotton glued on paper.

Try making some yarn pictures on the burlap or on a rug remnant or a piece of felt. Yarn will stick to these materials easily because of their rough surfaces.

Yarn can be cut or ripped, or its individual threads can be untwisted. What else can you do with yarn?

A Yarn Painter

. . . was at work "painting" with yarn.
The yarn was frayed, ripped, cut, twirled,
and put into a variety of shapes to
make this picture.

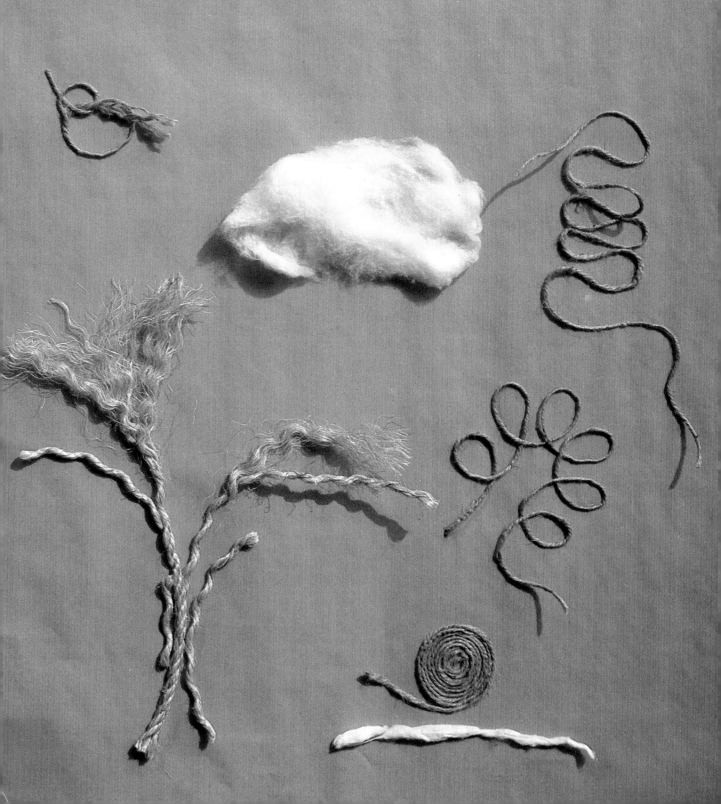

You will need:

Yarn, cloth scraps, cotton, felt, cardboard, fake pearls or beads, buttons, glue, scissors

1. Fold a piece of cloth in half and roll it.

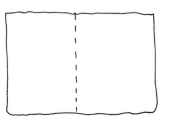

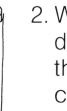

2. Wind a yarn dress around the rolled cloth.

3. You can wind a yarn hat around the top of the cloth.

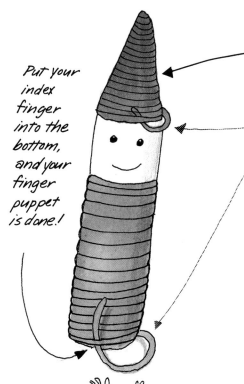

Put your index finger into the bottom, and your finger puppet is done!

4. To keep the yarn in place, stick the end under the last strand and put on some glue.

5. Paint on a face, or glue on some pearls or beads for eyes and a piece of yarn for the mouth.

6. For the sun, cut a circle from the cardboard. Glue short lengths of yarn around the edges. Cut another circle from felt and glue it to the cardboard. Make a face on the felt. Cut out a strip of felt and glue the ends to the back of the sun. Leave room enough to put your finger through the center of the strip.

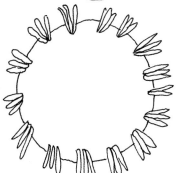

Maybe you can make a lion instead of a sun.

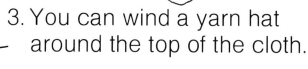

Finger Puppets

With cloth, beads, felt, and some yarn, you can make funny finger puppets. These puppets are fast and easy to make. You can make up your own stories, and your own finger-puppet theater can open its doors. Okay, raise the curtain!

You will need:

Different-colored yarn scraps, 1 cardboard tube from a paper-towel roll, glue, cardboard, 2 buttons, scissors, 2 long pieces of string

1. Spread glue over about one inch of the cardboard tube.

2. Wind yarn over the glue. Next, glue another inch of the tube and wind a different-color yarn around the glued area. Repeat the gluing and winding until the tube is covered.

3. When the tube has been completely covered, cut out a cardboard head and tail. Make slits on the dotted lines shown in the pictures. Slide the head on one end of the tube and the tail on the other. Cut out four legs and glue them onto the body. Glue a button on each side of the head for the eyes.

4. Do this with a friend. Thread two long strings through the tube. Now you and your friend should each wind the strings around the ends of your fingers as shown in the picture. Open your arms, and the dog will slide to your friend. When your friend opens his or her arms, the dog will slide back to you.

Zipping Pup

This colorful puppy will zip back and forth between two friends. But he can't decide which friend to play with.

You will need:

Different-colored yarn, construction paper, lots of nice small things to hide in your yarn wrappings

This is how you make a ball of yarn:

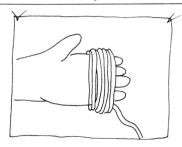

Wind the yarn several times around four fingers of one hand. Push it off your fingers, then wind more yarn in the opposite direction around the yarn you took off your fingers. Keep on winding the yarn in both directions until you have a round ball.

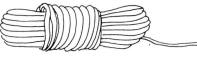 

Take the end of the yarn and put it under some of the outer threads so that it will not unwind.

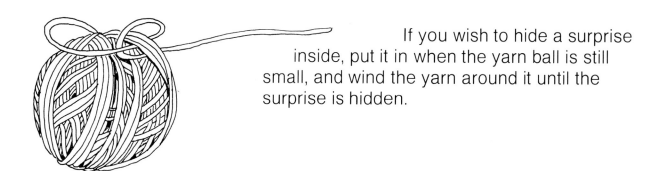

If you wish to hide a surprise inside, put it in when the yarn ball is still small, and wind the yarn around it until the surprise is hidden.

If you like, you can decorate the yarn ball with a ribbon or a hat.

To make a hat, cut out a circle from construction paper. Cut along the dotted line shown in the drawing. Overlap the edges of the cut until you have a cone shape. Then glue.

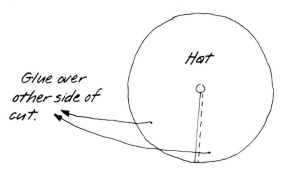

Glue over other side of cut.

Hat

Happy birthday!

What can I do with a ball of yarn?

Yarn Surprises

You can hide little presents in a yarn ball. A new idea in gift wrapping!

Imagine what fun it will be to open a present wrapped like this.

You will need:

Clear contact paper, yarn, scissors, needle and thread

Contact-paper decorations can be made all year round, whenever you like: for Halloween, for Christmas, or in the summer.

I'll make new pictures at Eastertime.

The big picture on the right shows winter decorations.

1. Cut a piece of clear contact paper to the desired size, and lay it in front of you with the protective paper facing up.

2. Carefully pull the protective paper off the contact sheet and begin making your designs with yarn on the sticky side.

Be sure the edges stay free of decoration. You can stick the paper directly on a window. Do the same with the ice flower.

3. For the ice flower, cut two flower shapes from the contact paper. Make your yarn design on one sticky surface and stick the other contact paper on top to seal your design. Cut evenly with the scissors. With the needle and thread, make a loop for hanging on the window.

You can make a window picture on any translucent material, such as Plexiglas.

Window Pictures

If your windows need decorations, make them from contact paper and yarn.

Ice flowers can cheer up your windows in the winter, until real flowers begin to bloom.

I'll make a princess.

You will need:
Several balls of yarn, assorted colors of scrap yarn, cardboard, cloth scraps, cotton, 2 sticks, scissors, beads and buttons for decoration

1. Put a cotton ball on the end of a stick and shape it so that it resembles a head. Wrap it with yarn.

3. For the arms, wind yarn around four fingers ten times. Push the yarn off your fingers and wind more yarn around it as shown.

2. When the head is made, push the stick through two yarn balls. Wind some yarn tightly around the bottom so that the two balls can't slip off.

Sew on here.

4. The arms are sewn to the body.

5. To make hair for the princess, wind yarn around a piece of cardboard. Put a thread through the top of the loops, draw the loops together loosely, and knot. Cut the loops at the bottom. Glue the hair to the top of the head.

★ Up to direction number 4, both dolls are made in the same way.

6. The prince has a turban instead of hair. Take a loose ball of yarn and wind some more yarn tightly around the middle of the ball. Decorate both puppets with beads, buttons, and cloth scraps.

16

Prince and Princess

You can decorate your puppets with
beads and sequins. With yarn and cloth
scraps, you can make a prince and princess
for your own fairy-tale theater:
Once upon a time . . .

You will need:

1 large colored piece of poster board, scissors, glue, a cotton ball, 2 beads, lots of yarn scraps, thin elastic

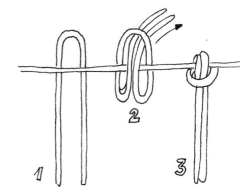

From poster board cut out a large circle and two ears.

Cut a V out of the circle (see the drawing).

Glue point A over point B.

Glue on the ears. Cut two holes for your eyes. Use the cotton ball for a nose.

Tie some elastic to the sides.

To make a yarn beard:

Tie a long piece of yarn between two chairs. Next, cut some short yarn threads:

1. Loop a thread behind the long yarn.

2. Take bottom ends over yarn and through top loop.

3. Pull the two ends down.

If the yarn is too thin, use a double strand.

When the beard is finished, glue it around the bottom of the mask.

You can do many other things with knotted yarn.

Yes, you can even make a skirt or a doll dress.

Maybe you have other ideas.

Monster Mask

Want to pretend to be a monster? Use poster board to make this mask with its crazy yarn beard.

You will need:

Yarn, cotton batting, buttons,
needle and thread, scissors,
felt-tip markers

1. Think about how your yarn animal
   might look. Big or small? Fat or thin?

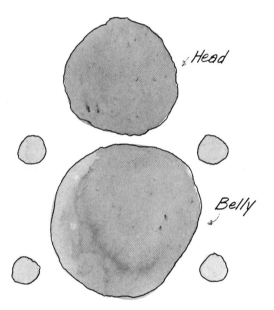

Head

Belly

2. Shape cotton into a head
   and a body.

3. Wind yarn loosely
   around each cotton ball
   and sew them together.

☆ Sew the yarn balls tightly
   together with a big needle.

4. Wind yarn around cotton to form four small balls
   for arms and legs. Sew these on too. A cat would
   need a tail also.

5. You still need eyes and a nose for each animal.
   Sew or glue on buttons for eyes. The bear can
   have a yarn-wrapped cotton ball for its nose.

It's fun to cuddle.

Woolly Max and
Cuddly Susie

Do you like cuddly animals?
They are best when you've made them yourself.
Choose some really nice soft yarn to make
cuddly animals in any size and color you like.
Got any ideas yet?

You will need:

Yarn, scissors, wire or pipe cleaners, tissue paper, safety pin

To make the flower: Depending on how thick the yarn is, wind it around your index and middle fingers three to six times. Remove the wound yarn and tie it together in the middle.

Half a flower is complete.

Two halves make a whole.

We made stems for the flowers from pipe cleaners. Cut leaves from tissue paper. Wind yarn around the stems and over the bottom tips of the tissue-paper leaves to attach the leaves to the stems.

You can tie a bunch of the flowers together for a bouquet, or you might pin one on your shirt or sweater.

"Plant" your yarn flowers in a pot or let them "bloom" outside in the snow.

22

Ever-Blooming Flowers

Even if it's winter outside and no real
flowers are blooming,
your yarn flowers will bloom
to cheer you up.
You might want to sprinkle some
perfume on your yarn flowers.

You will need:

A square piece of burlap, yarn scraps, beads, feathers, sticks, a needle, scissors, strings

You can experiment a lot with burlap—cut holes, pull out threads, glue on some decorations.

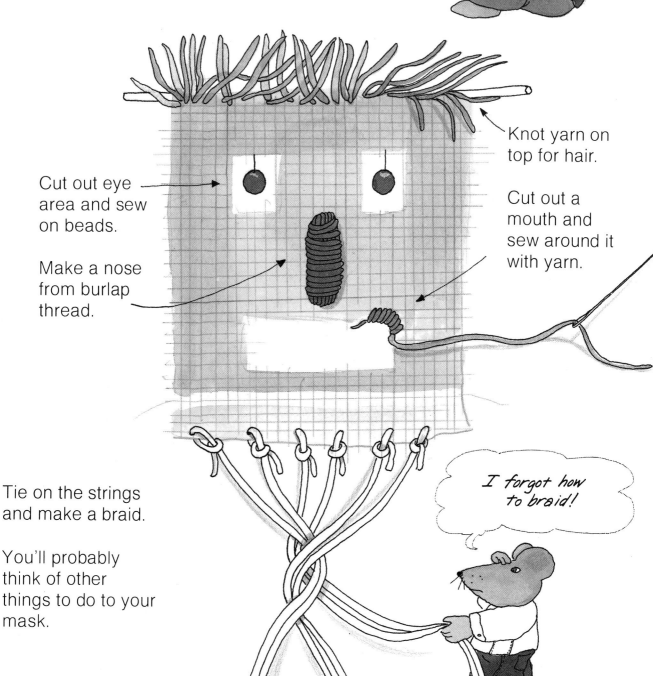

Knot yarn on top for hair.

Cut out eye area and sew on beads.

Cut out a mouth and sew around it with yarn.

Make a nose from burlap thread.

Tie on the strings and make a braid.

You'll probably think of other things to do to your mask.

I forgot how to braid!

Burlap Mask

Burlap is woven loosely.
You can poke holes
through it with your finger.
You can pull out the
threads. It is easy to
decorate. Be creative.
Try out your ideas.

Indoor Yarn Hopscotch Game

When it's raining, you can play outdoor games indoors. Use some yarn to make hopscotch games you can play on a rug.

Look! I've made a circle for my marble game.

I have a good idea: a toss game made from yarn.

Rules

Roll the yarn ball and try to make it land, in order, in each of the squares. If you miss, you have to start all over again.

4
3
2
1

You can make a train on the floor. Anyone who wants to ride in one of the train cars can try to hit the center of one of the cars. If the ball lands in the car, the player gets a ride.

You will need:

Notebooks, a calendar, small books, loose-leaf notebooks, envelopes, 3″ x 5″ cards, clear plastic folder. Then, depending on what you want to do to decorate: clear contact paper, yarn, cloth scraps, scissors, glue

You decide how and what to decorate.

Ideas

1. Cut a piece of clear contact paper, remove the protective covering, and make a yarn picture on the sticky surface. Then glue it on a notebook.

2. Make a yarn picture and glue it on a card.

3. The clear plastic folder can be decorated inside and outside.

4. Cut an opening in the notebook cover and make a window with the contact paper and the yarn.

I'll send this to my aunt.

I've stuck a picture on my loose-leaf notebook. I'll know right away it's mine.

Decorating
With Yarn

Notebooks, cards, and books look much more attractive and personal when decorated with yarn pictures. You need yarn, clear contact paper, scissors, and whatever else you might like to decorate with.

You will need:
Yarn, cotton, cardboard, scissors, glue, string, a box, paint and a paintbrush, pipe cleaner, construction paper

First make a lion.
(See page 20 for the body and the legs.)

The lion's face: Cut a circle from the cardboard and paint it yellow.

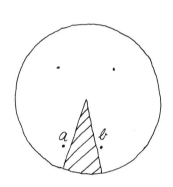

Cut out the triangle shape between A and B (see the drawing). Glue point A onto point B.

The mane: Make it from pieces of yellow yarn. The mane can be glued directly onto the head, or you can do it as shown on the large mask on page 24.

Sew or glue the head to the body. Make the tail from a pipe cleaner wrapped with yarn.

The lion cage:

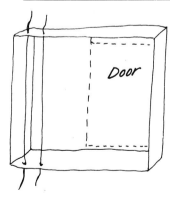

With a thick needle, thread the string from the top to the bottom of the box. Knot the ends on top and bottom. Cut a door in the back of the box. Make four wheels and glue them on. Paint the cage. Make more cages for other animals—for tame tigers and wild mice.

A Good Lion

Every day the lion performs
in the circus. But now he's
resting in this comfortable
cage. Wouldn't you like
a lion just like this?
See the page at left
for directions.

You will need:
A lid from a large shoe or boot box, string, different-colored yarn, scissors, a large needle

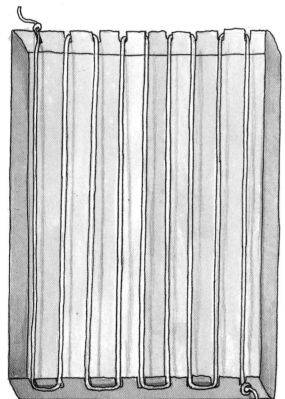

Cut an equal number of slots on the two short sides of the box lid.

Knot the string at one end and weave it tightly back and forth through the slots, as shown in the drawing.

Thread the yarn into a large needle and weave the yarn back and forth through the string to create your picture.

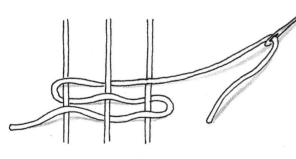

First think about what you want to weave and what colors you want to use. Maybe you'll just weave a pattern.

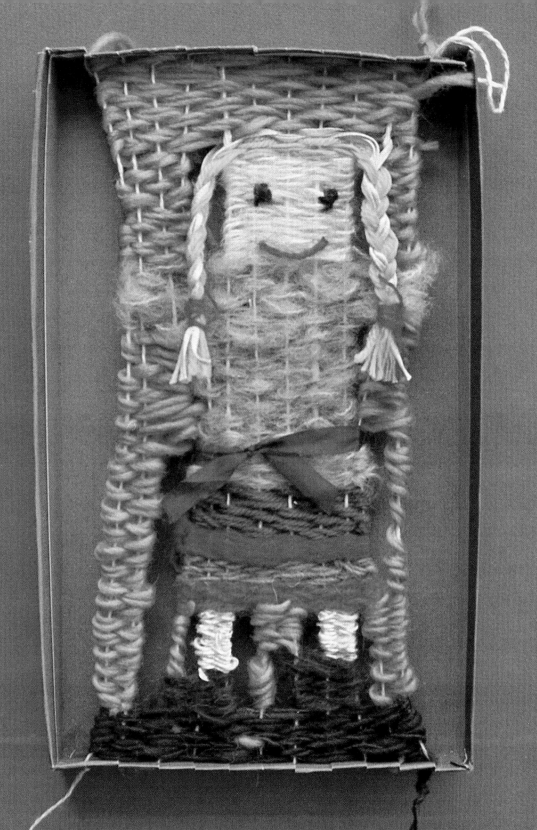

Woven Picture

You've probably painted a lot of pictures with paint. But have you ever woven a picture with yarn? It's really not difficult.

You will need:

A cardboard tube from a paper-towel roll, yarn for the sheep, cotton batting, cardboard, scissors, glue, straight pins with black heads, wooden sticks for the fence

Cut the cardboard tube in half; use one half for each sheep. Make a head-shaped ball of cotton and glue it to one end of the tube. Wrap yarn around the cotton ball and the end of the tube as shown in the drawing.

Use pins for eyes.

Glue on cardboard ears.

Cut four legs from cardboard and glue them to the tube. Then the sheep can stand up.

Use unraveled yarn for one sheep. You can unravel the yarn by untwisting the strands. The white sheep can have straight hair. To make the hair, wrap yarn around a piece of cardboard about 5 inches wide. Tie a string around the wrapped yarn at one end of the cardboard. Now cut through all the strands of yarn at the other end of the cardboard. Then glue the tied top to the sheep's body.

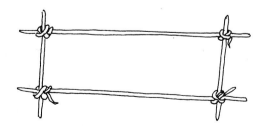

To make the fence, you need four sticks, two long and two short. Knot them together with yarn as in the drawing.

A Pair of Sheep

One sheep has curly hair and one has nice
straight hair. You might try to find some
unraveled yarn from an old sweater for
the curly hair. Directions for making
the sheep are on the opposite page.

You will need:

Small wooden sticks, glue, yarn, scissors, cardboard

Tepees:

Build a frame with three of the longer sticks and tie them together on top. Use three shorter sticks to tie to the bottom.

When the frame is done, wrap yarn around it. Put glue on the sticks before you wrap the yarn. Always put on some glue before the next layer of yarn is added.

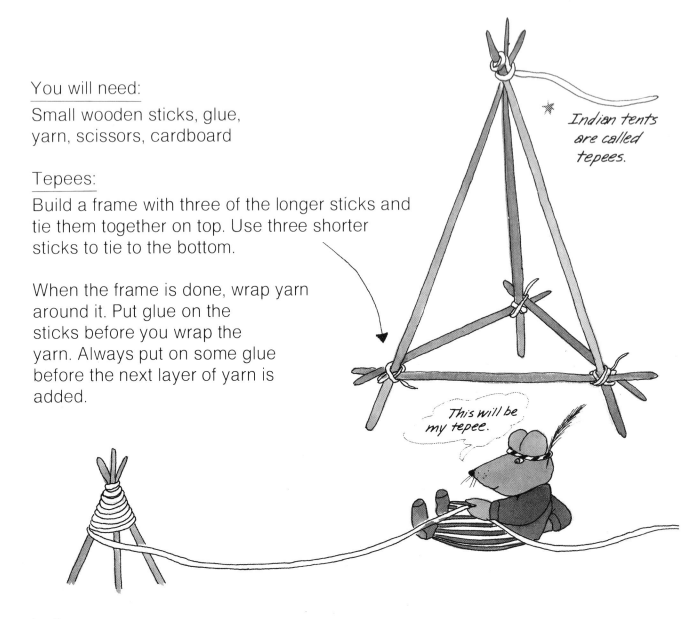

Indian tents are called tepees.

This will be my tepee.

Indians:

Wrap yarn around a 4-inch piece of cardboard. Wrap it around about ten or fifteen times. Take the yarn off the cardboard. Cut the loop open at one end. Tie a yarn thread around the loop near the top and braid two braids.

Make arms by cutting twelve equally long yarn threads. Put them around the Indian's body as the drawing shows, and braid these too.

Make the second arm just the way you made the first—only attach it on the other side.

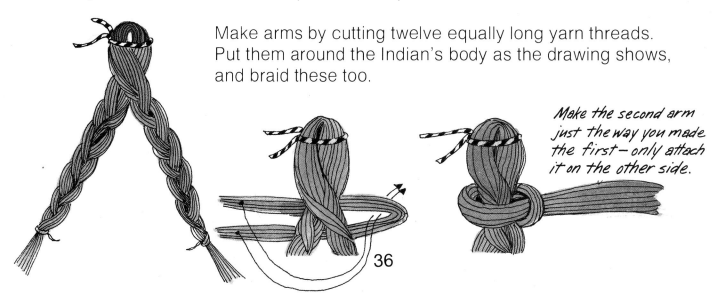

36

Indian Village

Indian tents are called tepees. Use small sticks
wrapped with yarn to make the tepees.
People are made by braiding the yarn.

You will need:

Yarn remnants, a net shopping bag or some net material,
scissors, a safety pin

Thick yarn is best because the weaving goes faster.

I'll double the yarn.

1. Cut a long piece of yarn. Pull the yarn through the safety pin and knot the ends together.

2. Weaving is done by pulling the safety pin threaded with yarn through the shopping-bag net, over and under.

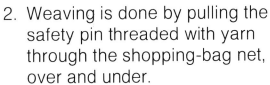

It is easier if you put a piece of paper in the bag!

Weave whatever you like: figures, patterns, horizontal or vertical.

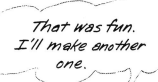

That was fun. I'll make another one.

You can knot the yarn directly in the net.

Lay the yarn as shown at (1) in the picture. Then push the two ends through the loop as in (2). Pull the ends tight.

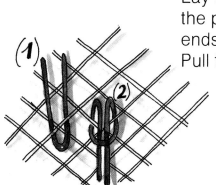

Net Shopping Bag

Oranges are sometimes sold in net bags. Nice pictures can be woven into the latticework of the net. If you can't get a net bag, use any net material.

You will need:

Cardboard, a pencil, yarn, scissors, a large needle, colored paper for eyes and beaks, glue

You can make all kinds of animals out of yarn pom-poms.

1. Cut two equal-size doughnut shapes out of cardboard. Put one circle on top of the other. Thread the needle with yarn and start wrapping yarn around the cardboard, as shown in the drawing. Keep wrapping until the circles are completely covered with yarn.

Use the bottom of a glass to get even circles.

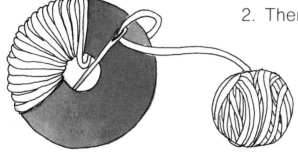

2. Then cut the yarn on the outer edge.

3. After you cut the yarn, carefully pull the two cardboard circles apart a little bit and tie the center very tightly with yarn. Cut the cardboard circles so that they can be removed. There is your pom-pom!

Cut cardboard feet and glue them on.

What kind of animal would you like to make?

I made a mouse!

40

A Little Zoo

So far we have one owl, one pink
jungle bird, and one big caterpillar.
But these three would like
companions. Make more animals
and it will be a big zoo!

You will need:

An old sock, cardboard, scissors, yarn remnants, 2 buttons, needle, thread, glue

Take the sock and cut it on the lines shown in the drawing.

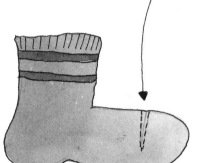

With needle and thread, sew around the cut in the sock so that it will not come unraveled.

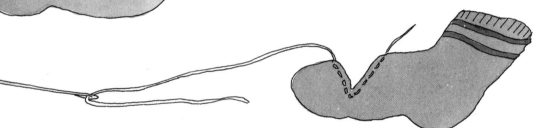

Cut a round piece of cardboard the size of the hole in the sock and bend it in the middle.

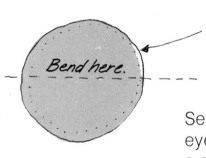

Put glue on the edge of the cardboard circle and stick it into the hole in the sock.

Sew yarn hair and button eyes on the sock. Fasten a string with a pom-pom on one end to the bottom of the mouth.

Pull the sock over your hand, and try to catch the pom-pom with your snapping sock.

Snapping Sock

This greedy stocking animal won't frighten
anyone! Do you have an old sock?
Then you can make this fun creature.

You will need:

Yarn remnants, thin wooden sticks, scissors, thick cardboard

Tie two sticks together at their centers, forming a cross.

Wrap different-colored yarn around all the sticks as shown in the drawings.

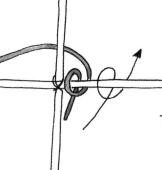

Wrap yarn evenly once or twice around each stick.

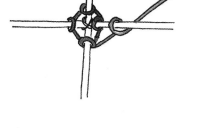

Knot the ends of yarn tightly, so that it won't come undone.

I'll try this with four sticks.

Stick a God's-eye into a heavy piece of cardboard as the sail of your sailboat.

Native Americans (Indians) made these God's-eyes, but they called them Magic Eyes.

44

God's-eye
Sailboats

You will need:
Yarn, scissors

This is how you make a variety of strings and cords!

Crocheting with fingers—chain stitch

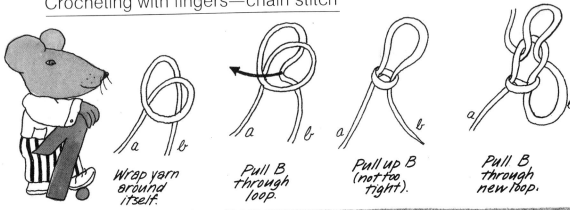

Wrap yarn around itself.

Pull B through loop.

Pull up B (not too tight).

Pull B through new loop.

Braided rope

Tie ends.

Braid a rope out of pieces of yarn and tie securely at both ends.

Twisted cord

This is best done by two people.

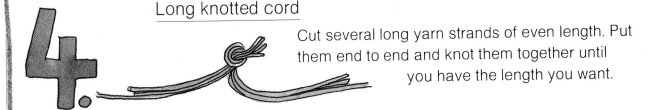

Each person takes one end of a double length of yarn in hand. Each person turns the yarn in the opposite direction from the other, until the yarn is tightly wound. Then lay a closed scissors in the center of this twisted yarn so that it won't unwind. Tie a knot in each end of the cord. Trim the ends.

Long knotted cord

Cut several long yarn strands of even length. Put them end to end and knot them together until you have the length you want.

Colorful knotted band

Take different-colored yarn pieces of an even length. Lay them beside each other and make knots at even intervals.

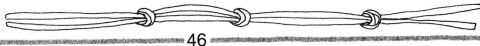

Strings and Ribbons

Yarn can be braided, twisted, or knotted! See the opposite page for directions.

Short Lesson in Threads and Fibers

Yarn is thread made from various fibers that have been twisted very tightly. Yarns can be made from animal hair, plant fiber, or synthetic fibers. There are even shiny threads made out of minerals.

Animal fibers

1. Wool is what we call fibers that come from animals. Sheep wool comes from sheep.

2. Cashmere wool comes from cashmere goats.

3. Mohair comes from the Angor goat.

4. Alpaca comes from llamas.

5. Camel-hair wool comes from camels.

6. Cuddly angora wool comes from rabbits.

You can tell the difference between various yarns by touch.

Plant fibers

Examples of plant fibers are cotton (1), flax (2), hemp (3), and jute (4).

Synthetic fibers are made chemically.
There are also mixed animal-plant-synthetic fibers.

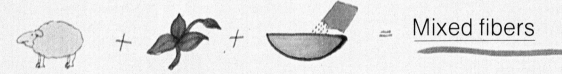 = Mixed fibers

And don't forget the shiny metal fibers made from various minerals.

Gosh! That was an exhausting lesson!

You will need:

Heavy cardboard, scissors, glue, red paper, yarn, a button, paper fastener

Cut a hedgehog shape out of heavy cardboard.

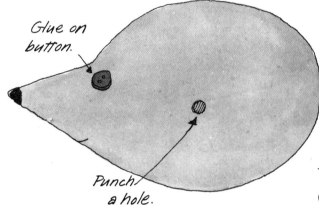

Glue on button.

Punch a hole.

Make a half pom-pom out of yarn. (See page 40 for pom-pom directions.)

To make legs for the hedgehog, draw a circle on cardboard. Draw legs that look like this. Cut out around the legs.

"Shoes" are cut out of red paper and glued on the feet.

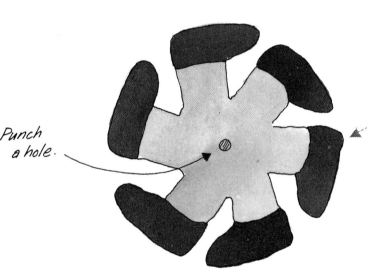

Punch a hole.

Lay the body on top of the legs so that the two holes line up. Push the paper fastener through the two holes and fasten it. Glue the pom-pom to the body. Paper fastener goes here.

When you hold the top of your hedgehog and move him forward, his legs will move in a way that will make him look as if he's really walking.

Walking Hedgehog

You will need:

Yarn, scissors, glue, a large
piece of cardboard or burlap

Other things for your pictures: tree bark, leaves, beads,
buttons, cotton batting, colored construction paper

Think about what you would like to make.

A Tree?

The tree can be made with many yarn pom-poms
(see page 40).

A Bird?

Wrap two yarn balls and glue them together. Make
wings and a beak from construction paper.

Try some other ideas!

Do this with friends. It can be fun. Each person
makes something different. Then you glue everything
together into one big picture.

If you want your pictures to stand up, cut out a long
strip of cardboard and glue it to the back.

Glue cardboard
on back.

I'll put the tree
in this box and paint
in a background.

A Giant Picture

Working with friends is the most fun.

Each person makes something from yarn: animals, trees, houses, clouds.

Then glue everything to a large piece of cardboard or a piece of burlap.

You will need:
Yarn in different colors,
scissors

This is how to knit with
your fingers.

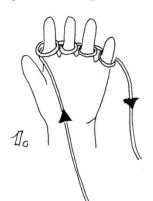

Wrap the yarn in loose
loops around your
fingers.

1.

*Pull loop over
fingers to the
back of your hand.*

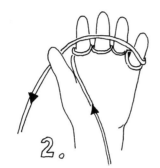

2.

Next, put the yarn from
the front over the loops.
Let the yarn between
your thumb and index
finger hang down in back.

Starting with your index finger, pull each
loop over the top of the finger to the
back. Do one finger at a time until you
have finished the row.

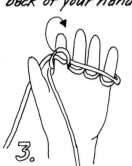

3.

*If you have to
stop while knitting,
just push the stitches
onto a wooden cooking-
spoon handle until you
are ready to start again.*

Then put the yarn over the back of your
hand, past the little finger, and again over
the loops (as in 2).

After five or six rows, pull on the lowest row and you can see
that you are knitting a tube.

Knit as long as you want until your scarf is long enough for
you. Knit many different-colored tubes of the same length.

Sew the tubes together, or just knot them together, as shown
in the picture on the right.

*I think
this scarf
is too long.*

A Long, Colorful Scarf

Knitting with your fingers is not hard to do. Once you know how, you can knit lots of long scarves.

To knit the mouse mittens shown in the picture at the right, you must build a small knitting machine.

You will need:

A strip of heavy, flexible cardboard about 4 inches wide and 10 inches long, masking tape, 14 nails about 2½ inches long with big heads, yarn, scissors, knitting needle, felt-tip marker, thin elastic, 2 beads

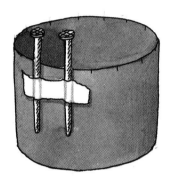

Roll up and tape the cardboard so that you have a tube about 3 inches in diameter. Make fourteen marks evenly around the tube. With tape, attach the nails, one at each mark, so that the heads are about ½ inch above the tube. Then wrap yarn over the nails. Keep the beginning of the yarn visible for knotting together with the end later.

Here is how to knit.

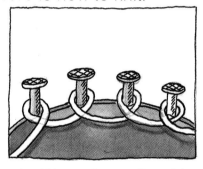

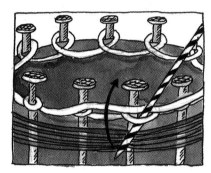

1. Wrap the nails with yarn. Do it with the same kind of yarn you will use for knitting later.

2. When all the nails are wrapped, lead the yarn along the outside of the tube.

3. With a thin knitting needle lift the stitch and lead it over the nail toward the back. Do this with each nail, around and around. Hold the thread loosely, otherwise the stitches will be too tight.

If you want to finish your knitting, pull the end of the yarn through each stitch as before, but lift it out of the nail this time.

Knit the last three rows in pink for the mouse's mouth, pulling the yarn together tightly.

Roll up some yarn for the ears and sew them on. Use beads for the eyes.

Pull a thin elastic through here.

Don't forget the whiskers.

These mice can
keep your
hands warm.

You will need:
Two wooden hangers, one ball of string, paint to color the wooden hangers, scissors

1. Cut ten even pieces of string about 2 yards long.

2. Double each string and loop them on one of the hangers (see the drawing), making sure to space them evenly.

Always knot one complete row before you go on to the next row.

3. Hang the hanger so that the strings hang down. Knot the string as shown in the picture.

Row 1 →

Row 2 →

a a b b c c

a a b b c c

When you have knotted all the strings to the end, tie them to the other hanger.

This takes awhile to do.

How long do I still have to wait?

Pull a string through each outside edge of the hammock, and tie the ends of the strings to the hangers.

58

Teddy Bear's Hammock

It's fun to swing in a hammock. Have you ever done it?
Big hammocks are made the same way as this little one.
Naturally, it is much faster to make a small hammock.

You will need:

Yarn remnants, a big shoe or boot box, glue, a cardboard tube from a toilet-paper roll, a small box, scissors, cardboard, skewers

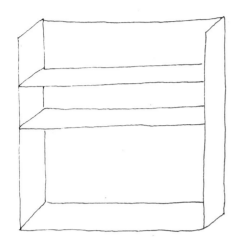

Make the store from the shoe box

Glue two cardboard strips to the sides for shelves. A small empty box will be the counter. Make some signs for your store. Make lots of small yarn balls for your shelves.

Here is a different way to roll up yarn:

Cut an H shape out of cardboard and wrap yarn around the middle. Fasten the end in a small cut in the

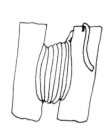

cardboard so that it doesn't come loose.

The salesperson is a yarn-wrapped cardboard tube. The head is made with pink yarn. The hair is yarn cut and glued to the head. To make arms, double up several strands of yarn, wind more yarn around the strands, and glue the arms to the body.

Use skewers for knitting needles in the store.

Ann's Yarn Shop

"What do I do with so many leftover pieces of yarn?"
Ann asked herself. Then she had an idea:
She set up a little yarn shop in an old shoe box.
Maybe you would like to have one too.

Boo!

You will need:

White yarns (cotton, wool, etc.), some red and black yarn for the eyes and mouth, cardboard, scissors, glue

1. Wind one kind of white yarn around a rectangle of cardboard.

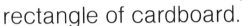

Pull this thread

through.

Over this white yarn, wind another sort of white yarn. For example, first use white cotton yarn and next mohair or wool yarn or whatever you have.

2. When you decide your ghost is thick enough, pull a long thread under and through the wound yarn.

Cut open here.

Tie it tightly at the top. Then cut the yarn at the bottom of the cardboard.

3. Cut the top yarn layer for hair. Glue on eyes and a mouth.

The hair is too long.

The bigger the cardboard, the bigger your ghosts will be.

62

Ghost Hour

These little ghosts won't scare you.
They are soft and cuddly and you
can make them yourself!

INDEX